# Wonders

Mc
Graw
Hill
Education

**Cover and Title Page:** Nathan Love

**www.mheonline.com/readingwonders**

Send all inquiries to:
McGraw-Hill Education
2 Penn Plaza
New York, NY 10121


ISBN: 978-0-02-132448-4
MHID: 0-02-132448-4

Printed in the United States of America.

9 LKV 25                                    D

# Wonders

# ELD
## Companion Worktext

**Program Authors**

Diane August

Jana Echevarria

Josefina V. Tinajero

McGraw Hill Education

# Unit 3

# Getting from Here to There

**The Big Idea**

# Getting from Here to There

# The Big Idea

What kinds of experiences can lead to new discoveries?

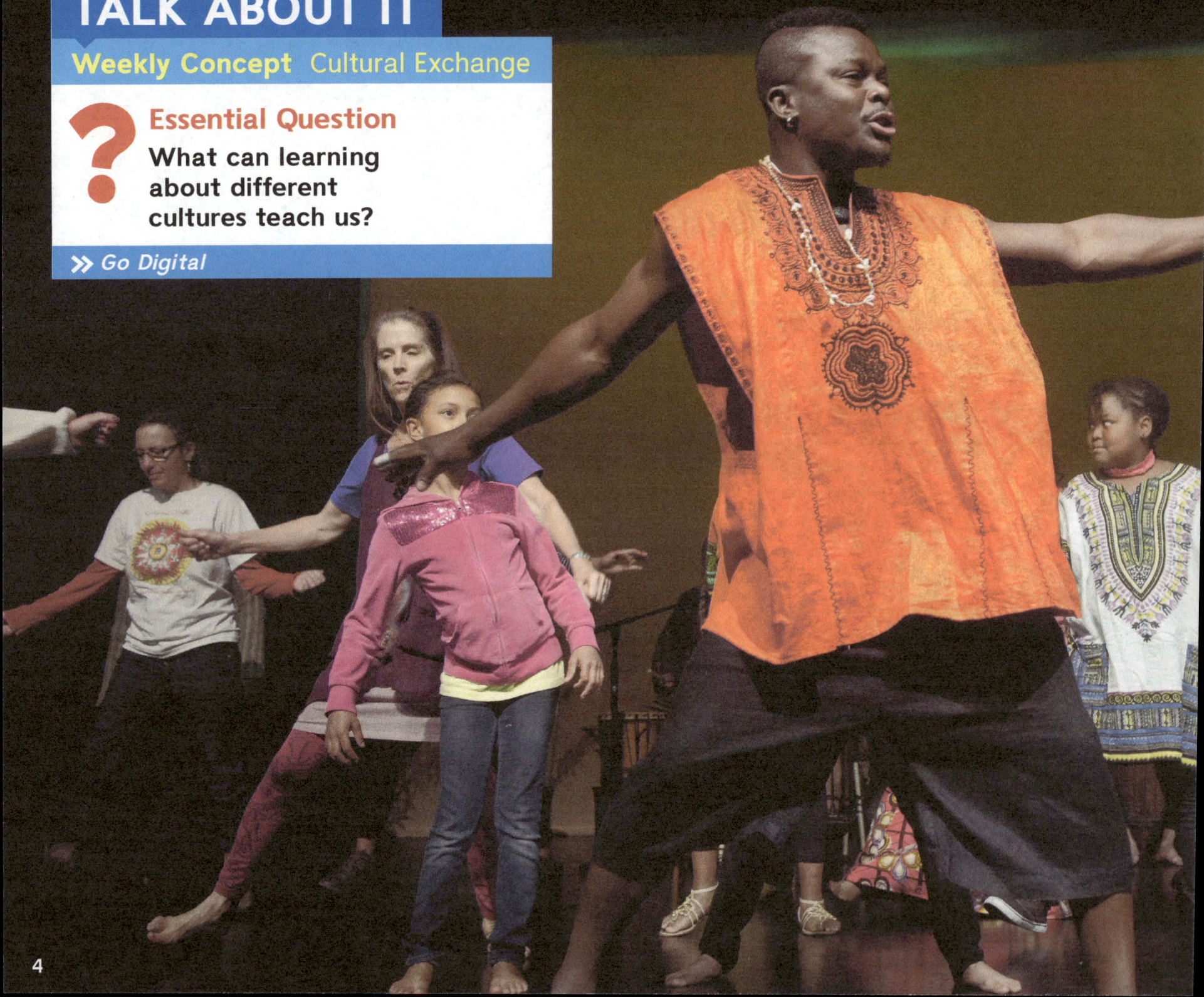

**?** **Essential Question**

What can learning about different cultures teach us?

>> *Go Digital*

**What is the woman teaching her students? What do you learn from a different culture? Write your ideas in the chart.**

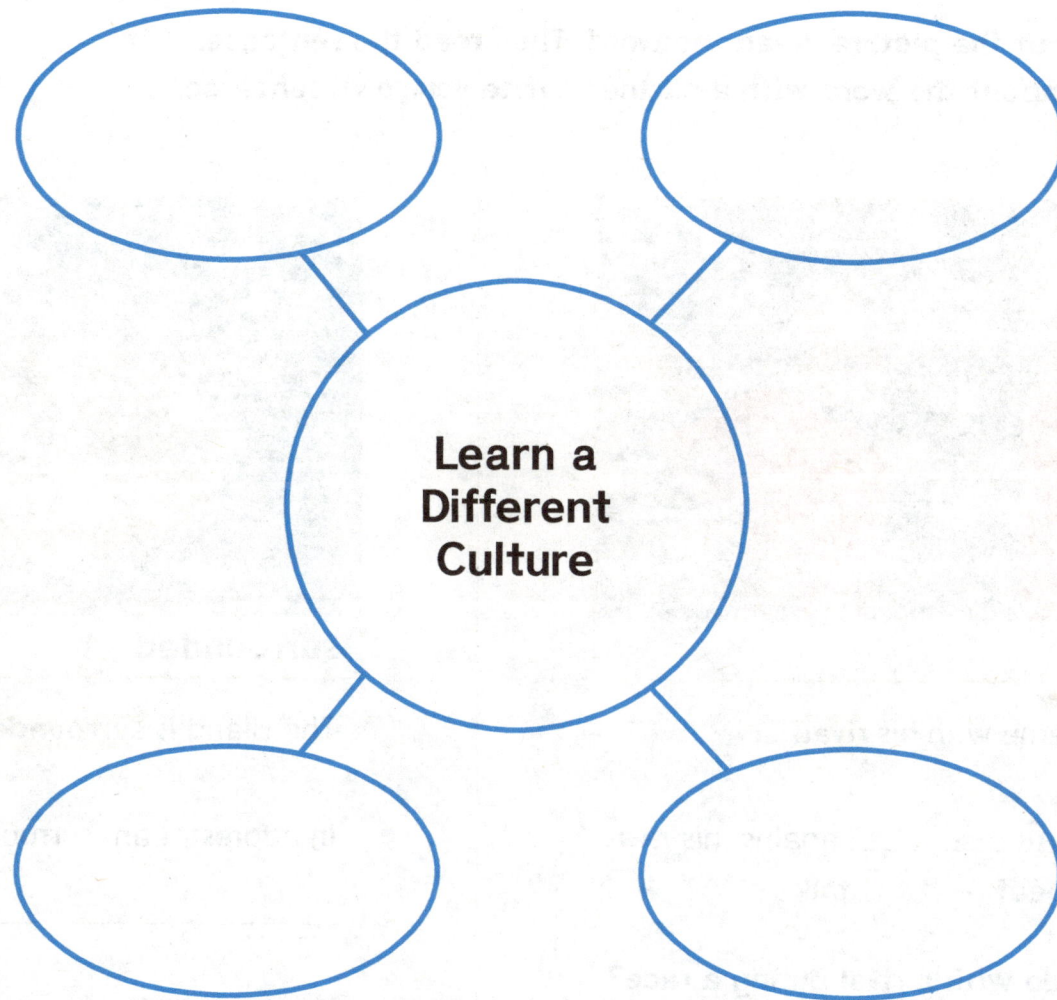

COLLABORATE

Learn a Different Culture

**Discuss what different cultures teach you. Use words from the chart. You can say:**

Different cultures teach me about _____

_____.

# More Vocabulary

Look at the picture. Read the word. Then read the sentence.
Talk about the word with a partner. Write your own sentence.

**rival**

Max plays a game with his **rival**.

Max wants to _____ against his *rival*.
**win**          **meet**          **talk**

**What do you do with a rival during a race?**

I _____ against my rival.

**surrounded**

The island is **surrounded** by water.

In a forest, I am surrounded by _____

_____.

**Who are you surrounded by in a classroom?**

In a classroom, I am surrounded by _____

_____.

# Words and Phrases: *break*

One meaning of the word *break* is "a vacation."

When does the family go fishing?

The family goes fishing during the summer **break**.

Another meaning of *break* is "a short rest."

Why are the runners sitting on the track?

The runners are taking a **break** during their practice.

**Talk with a partner. Look at the picture. Read the sentence. Circle the meaning of the underlined word.**

The students went to the playground to take a break from their school day.

a short rest     a vacation

The children go camping during their summer break.

a short rest     a vacation

COLLABORATE

## 1 Talk About It

Look at the photographs. Read the title. Discuss what you see. Use these words.

**city   buildings   passport   travel**

Write about what you see.

The story is about a boy who _____

_____

_____ .

Where is the boy going?

He is going to _____

_____ .

What information does the map tell you?

The map shows _____

_____ .

Take notes as you read the story.

# A Reluctant TRAVELER

PASSPORT

United States of America

### Essential Question

**?**  **What can learning about different cultures teach us?**

Read about what Paul discovers in Argentina and what he learns about himself.

Paul and his family were going to Argentina to visit Aunt Lila and Uncle Art. Paul was sure it wasn't going to be a fun vacation. "It's weird to pack winter clothes in August," Paul said.

His mom contradicted Paul. She said, "It's not weird, honey. Argentina is in the Southern hemisphere, and we're in the Northern hemisphere, so the seasons are opposite."

Ever since Paul's aunt and uncle relocated to Argentina, Paul's parents had started collecting travel **guides**, full of cultural information. Paul's parents wanted an exciting vacation, but Paul wanted to stay in New York and play soccer with his friends during the summer break.

As the plane took off, Paul's father pointed down to New York and said, "Look, you can see the island of Manhattan **surrounded** by water." Many hours later, as the plane landed, Paul saw Buenos Aires. It had similar outlines of a city and bright lights everywhere, just like home.

Cartesia/Photodisc/Getty Images

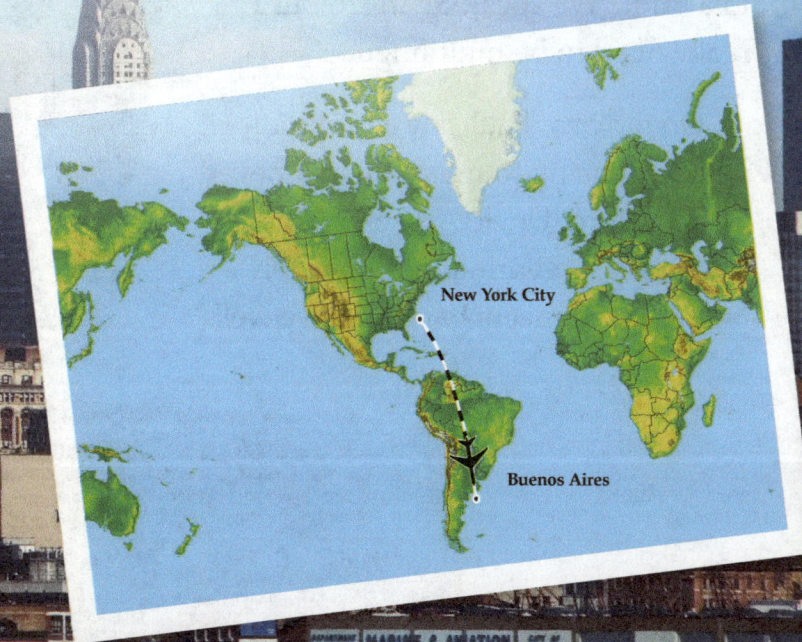

New York City

Buenos Aires

# Text Evidence

**1 Sentence Structure** (A)(C)(T)

Reread the second sentence. The sentence tells about what Paul was thinking about. Circle the text that tells you. Rewrite the sentence.

Paul thought the vacation _____

_____.

**2 Specific Vocabulary** (A)(C)(T)

*Guides* are books with information about a topic. Underline the text that tells the topic of the guides.

The guides have information about

_____.

**3 Comprehension**

Reread the last paragraph. How is Buenos Aires similar to New York City?

New York and Buenos Aires have

_____

_____.

9

# Text Evidence

## 1 Specific Vocabulary ACT

Reread the second paragraph. The phrase *take a taste* means to "try a little bit of food." Underline the text that tells why Paul's mom tells him to take a taste.

## 2 Sentence Structure ACT

Reread the last sentence in the third paragraph. Circle the two past-tense verbs. Underline the word that tells that two events happened at the same time.

## 3 Comprehension

Reread the last paragraph. What new thing does Paul learn about? Put a box around the text. How do you know that Paul is learning something new?

I know that Paul learned about

something new because _____

_____

_____.

At the airport, Aunt Lila greeted Paul's family warmly with hugs. Then they had dinner at a restaurant. Uncle Art ordered for everyone: *Empanadas* (small meat pies), *parrillada* (grilled meat), *chimichurri* (spicy sauce), and *ensalada mixta* (lettuce, tomatoes, and onions).

Paul frowned at all the new food. His mom said, "Just take a taste." Some of the spices and flavors were familiar to Paul.

Paul ate an empanada. He said, "This is really good. I had this at César's house." As Paul complimented the food, he felt his mood improve.

The first day in Buenos Aires was exciting. There were new sights, sounds, and languages. Paul saw that Buenos Aires had people from all over the world, similar to New York. Aunt Lila said, "We speak Spanish, but I really need to be multilingual."

On a plaza, Paul saw a group of people dancing to music he had never heard before. Uncle Art said, "That's the tango. Argentina is famous for tango. The dancers have to move well."

"The tango is pretty cool," Paul said.

Around noon, Paul's family drove to an unusual neighborhood. All the buildings were decorated yellow and blue. Aunt Lila said, "Soccer season has started!"

Paul was surprised. He thought it was winter in Argentina. He asked, "Isn't it too cold for soccer?"

Aunt Lila said, "It's nearly spring here. There is a game this afternoon at La Bombonera, the famous stadium." Aunt Lila showed Paul five tickets to the game. Paul looked amazed.

Uncle Art said, "We're in the neighborhood of La Bombonera. The neighborhood team Boca will play River, the rival team. So people decorate in Boca colors."

"Maybe I will paint my room in soccer team colors!" Paul said.

Paul's mom smiled and said, "I am proud of you, Paul! You're a great traveler."

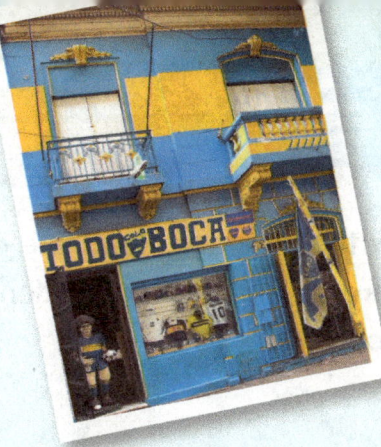

## Make Connections

**?** Talk about what Paul and his family learned about the culture of Argentina. What did Paul learn about himself? **ESSENTIAL QUESTION**

What has learning about a different culture taught you? **TEXT TO SELF**

# Text Evidence 🔍

## ❶ Specific Vocabulary Ⓐ Ⓒ Ⓣ

Reread the second paragraph. The word *unusual* has the prefix *un-* which means "not." Why was the neighborhood unusual? Underline the sentence that tells you.

**COLLABORATE**

## ❷ Talk About It

Reread the fifth paragraph. Discuss why people decorate the neighborhood in Boca colors.

People decorate in Boca colors

because _____

_____.

## ❸ Comprehension
### Theme

Before the trip, Paul didn't want to travel, but by the end of the trip he was a great traveler. How did the trip change Paul?

Paul learned _____

_____.

# Respond to the Text

**Partner Discussion** Work with a partner. Read the questions about "A Reluctant Traveler." Show where you found text evidence. Write the page numbers. Then discuss what you read.

---

**Why did Paul not want to go on a trip?**

I read that Paul wanted to spend his summer with _____

_____.

Paul didn't think the trip _____.

**Text Evidence** 🔍

Page(s): _____

Page(s): _____

---

**What did Paul learn about Argentina?**

I read that Paul tried _____.

At a plaza, Paul watched _____.

Paul visited a neighborhood _____

_____.

**Text Evidence** 🔍

Page(s): _____

Page(s): _____

Page(s): _____

---

**Group Discussion** Present your answers to the group. Cite text evidence for your thinking. Listen to and discuss the group's opinions.

**Write** Work with a partner. Look at your notes about "A Reluctant Traveler." Write your answer to the Essential Question. Use text evidence to support your answer. Use vocabulary words in your writing.

**What did Paul learn about himself when he visited Argentina?**

Paul learned that the food in Argentina is _____

_____ .

People in Argentina enjoy _____

_____ .

Paul learned that he liked to _____ because _____

_____ .

**Share Writing** Present your writing to the class. Discuss their opinions. Think about their ideas. Explain why you agree or disagree with their ideas.

I agree with _____ .

I do not agree because _____ .

# Write to Sources

Chen

**Take Notes About the Text** I took notes about the text on the idea web to answer the question: *What are some similarities between New York City and Buenos Aires?*

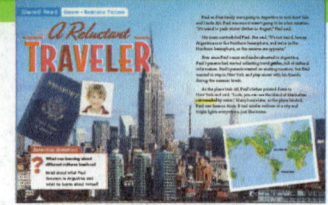

pages 8–11

**Detail**
Both cities are near an ocean.

**Detail**
Both cities are bright at night.

**Main Idea**
New York and Buenos Aires have similarities.

**Detail**
People in both cities cook with some of the same spices.

**Detail**
People in both cities eat some of the same foods.

Yobro10/iStock/360/Getty Images

14

**Write About the Text** I used notes from my idea web to write about similarities between New York and Buenos Aires.

## Student Model: *Narrative Text*

After the trip, Paul said to his mother, "I saw similarities between New York and Buenos Aires."

"What did you notice?" his mother asked.

Paul said, "Both cities are near an ocean. Both cities are bright at night."

"What else did you notice?" his mother asked.

He said, "People cook with the same spices. They also eat the same foods in both places."

## TALK ABOUT IT

COLLABORATE

### Text Evidence

**Underline** a supporting detail that comes from the notes. Which word tells you that the detail tells about a similarity?

### Grammar

**Circle** a verb in the present tense. Why did Chen use the present tense to tell about the cities?

### Connect Ideas

**Draw a box** around sentences that tell about both cities. How can you use the word *and* to connect the sentences?

### Your Turn

COLLABORATE

In the story, what is different about New York and Buenos Aires? Use text evidence in your writing.

>> *Go Digital!*
Write your response online. Use your editing checklist.

# TALK ABOUT IT

**Weekly Concept** Being Resourceful

 **Essential Question**
How can learning about
nature be useful?

**›› Go Digital**

How do the men collect the cranberries? Why is it useful to know about nature? Write your ideas in the chart.

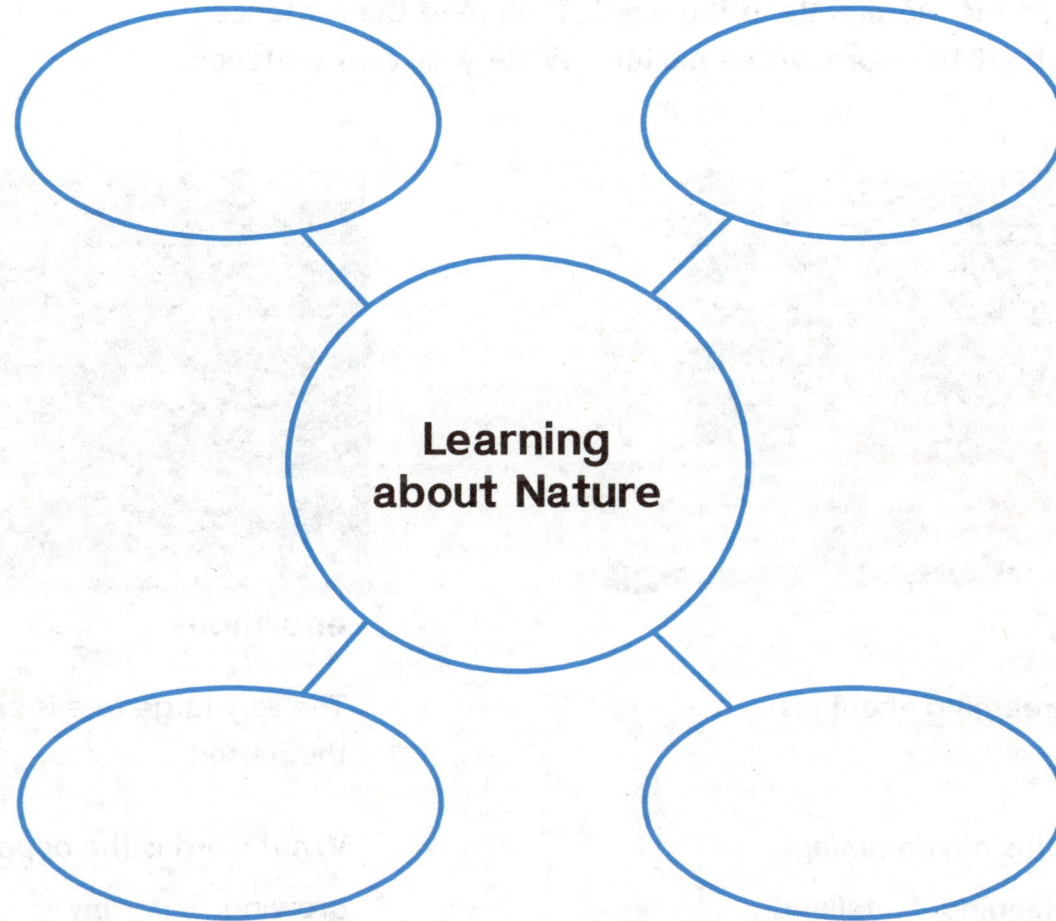

**Learning about Nature**

Discuss how learning about nature helped the men collect cranberries. Use words from the chart. Complete the sentences.

The men collect cranberries by _____.

It is useful to know about nature because _____

_____.

# More Vocabulary

**Look at the picture. Read the word. Then read the sentence. Talk about the word with a partner. Write your own sentence.**

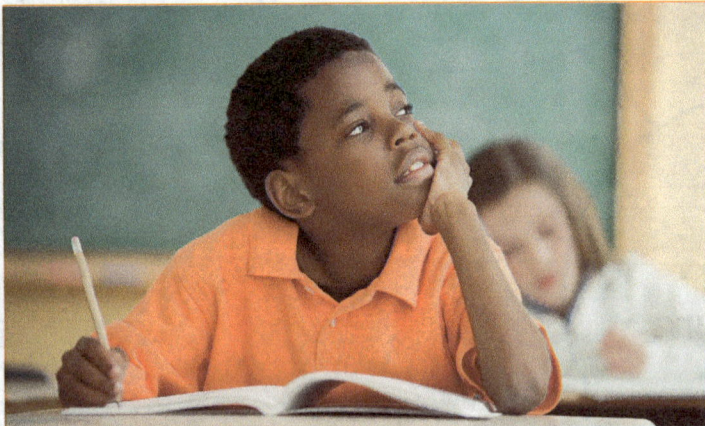

**daydreaming**

Tyrell was **daydreaming** about his baseball game.

What word means *daydreaming*?

**imagining    sleeping    talking**

**What happens when you are daydreaming?**

When I am daydreaming in class, I am not

_____ to the teacher.

**enormous**

The very large tree is **enormous** next to the person.

What word is the opposite of *enormous*?

**growing        tiny        scary**

**What animal is tiny? What animal is enormous?**

_____ is tiny, but

_____ is enormous.

18

# Words and Phrases: *must be* and *out of sight*

The phrase *must be* means "very possible that something is true."

How does Katy feel when she wins?

Katy **must be** happy.

The phrase *out of sight* means "something cannot be seen."

When the clouds appear, can you see the moon?

No, the moon is **out of sight.**

**COLLABORATE** Talk with a partner. Look at the picture. Read the sentence. Write the phrase that completes each sentence.

When the mouse hides in the hole, the mouse is _____.

      **must be**     **out of sight**

The woman _____ tired from running.

      **must be**     **out of sight**

# Survivaland

## 1 Talk About It

Look at the picture. Read the title. Talk about what you see. Use these words.

**computer   game   player
character   screen**

Write about what you see.

The story is about _____

_____

_____.

What are the children doing?

They are _____

_____.

What is on the computer screen?

The computer screen shows _____

_____.

Take notes as you read the story.

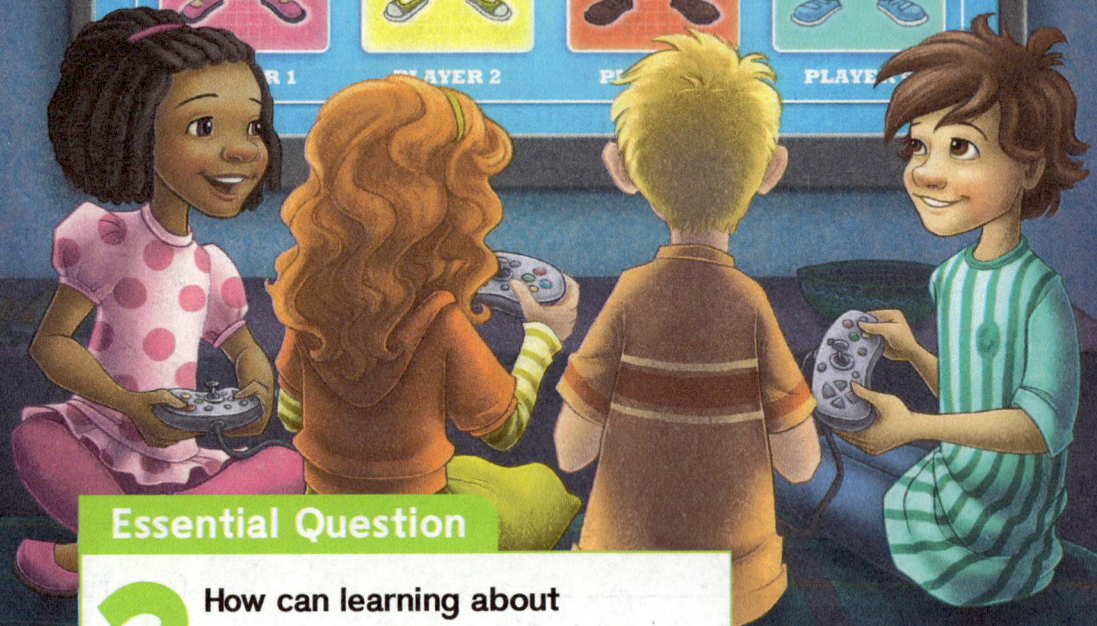

### Essential Question

**?**

**How can learning about nature be useful?**

Read how four friends use their knowledge of nature to survive.

"I will win *Survivaland*!" Raul declared and started the computer game. A character appeared on the screen. It started to run away from a sandstorm on a desert island.

Latrice warned, "Not today. I'll be the winner!" She moved her character on the screen.

Juanita insisted, "No way. I always devise a plan to win."

Jackson frowned, "This game is too complex. You have to know about nature, but that's not important in real life."

A loud *crackle* sounded and the room went dark. Suddenly the four players were on the computer screen. They were characters in the computer game!

Raul yelled, "We're inside the game! And the sandstorm is blinding me! What do we do?" Suddenly, they saw a large sign in the sky: RUN WEST TO ESCAPE THE STORM.

"Which way is west?" Jackson asked.

Latrice pointed to the sun and shouted, "The sun is rising over there. The sun rises in the east and sets in the west, so west must be opposite the sun."

Maryn Roos

# Text Evidence

### 1 Specific Vocabulary A C T

The word *declared* means "said what the person thinks or feels." What did Raul declare? Underline the text.

Raul declared that _____

_____.

### 2 Comprehension

Reread the fourth paragraph. What does Jackson say about nature in real life? Underline your answer.

Jackson thinks that it is not _____

_____.

### 3 Sentence Structure A C T

Reread the last sentence. The sentence has two parts. Which part tells a conclusion? Put a box around the text. What clues did Latrice use for the conclusion?

Latrice knows that _____

_____

_____.

# Text Evidence

## 1 Sentence Structure ⓐⓒⓣ

Reread the first sentence. When did the players stop running? Underline the text that tells you.

The players stopped running when

_____

_____ .

## 2 Specific Vocabulary ⓐⓒⓣ

The phrase *drove away* means "forced someone or something to leave." What drove away the butterfly? Underline the text. Rewrite the sentence.

The bitter taste of the onion _____

_____ .

## 3 Comprehension

Reread fifth and sixth paragraphs. Circle what happened when Raul was daydreaming. Why did Raul say Jackson is resourceful?

Raul said that because _____

_____ .

The four players ran west until the sandstorm was safely behind them. Suddenly Juanita shouted, "We have new trouble overhead!" A giant butterfly was hovering above them.

Raul saw onions growing nearby. He smashed an onion into four pieces, and said, "Rub this over yourselves!"

The giant butterfly landed its feet on Juanita. She screamed, and the butterfly quickly flew away. Juanita thought her screams scared the butterfly.

Raul explained, "It was the onion. Butterflies taste with their feet, so the bitter taste of the onion drove away the butterfly."

Jackson looked confused. "Butterflies taste with their feet?" he asked. Raul replied, "Yes, we learned that in science class last year."

Jackson admitted, "I was probably daydreaming that day. Raul, you're resourceful!"

Then an enormous crow landed near the four players. It said, "I'm hungry." Juanita threw her silver bracelet and ring as far as she could. The crow chased the jewelry, while the friends ran away.

When the bird was out of sight, Jackson asked, "Juanita, why did you throw away your jewelry?"

Juanita explained, "I read that crows are attracted to shiny objects, and it went after the jewelry instead of us!"

Raul looked at Jackson and said, "Knowing about nature has saved us again."

The four friends ran until they accidentally tripped over a log and landed in mud. The mud covered their faces, making it impossible for them to see. They heard a loud *crackle* again. When they wiped off the mud and opened their eyes, they were back in Raul's game room, in front of the computer screen!

Latrice cried, "We have returned!"

Raul wondered, "Who won the game?"

Jackson declared, "We all did, but I'm the biggest winner because I learned to appreciate nature."

"Right!" the friends exclaimed, as they wondered what game to play next.

Maryn Roos

## Make Connections

**?** Talk about how the friends used their knowledge of nature to get out of dangerous situations. ESSENTIAL QUESTION

How can you use information about nature to stay safe and healthy? TEXT TO SELF

# Text Evidence

**1 Sentence Structure** A C T

Reread the second paragraph. What does the pronoun *it* refer to? Circle the text. What did the crow do?

The crow _____

_____.

**2 Comprehension**
**Theme**

How did knowing about nature save the group? Write your answer.

Knowing about nature saved them

because _____

_____.

COLLABORATE
**3 Talk About It**

Discuss how Jackson learned to appreciate nature. Write about it.

Jackson learned to appreciate

nature by _____

_____.

23

# Respond to the Text

**Partner Discussion** Work with a partner. Read the questions about "Survivaland." Show where you found text evidence. Write the page numbers. Then discuss what you read.

COLLABORATE

---

**What problems did the players have when they were in the computer game?**

**Text Evidence** 🔍

First, they had to escape the _____.    Page(s): _____

Next, there was a giant _____.    Page(s): _____

Finally, there was a hungry _____.    Page(s): _____

---

**How did knowing about nature help them solve their problems?**

**Text Evidence** 🔍

Latrice figured out _____.    Page(s): _____

Raul helped the players escape _____.    Page(s): _____

Juanita knew the crow _____.    Page(s): _____

---

**Group Discussion** Present your answers to the group. Cite text evidence for your thinking. Listen to and discuss the group's opinions.

COLLABORATE

**Write** Work with a partner. Look at your notes about "Survivaland." Write your answer to the Essential Question. Use text evidence to support your answer. Use vocabulary words in your writing. Then discuss what you read.

**How was knowing about nature useful to the players?**

The players had a problem because _____

_____.

While in the computer game, the players helped each other by _____

_____

_____.

At the end, Jackson declared _____

_____

_____.

**Share Writing** Present your writing to the class. Discuss their opinions. Think about their ideas. Explain why you agree or disagree with their ideas.

I agree with _____.

I do not agree because _____.

# Write to Sources

Miguel

**Take Notes About the Text** I took notes about the text on the chart to answer the question: *In your opinion, what is the most important lesson Jackson learned? Why do you think that?*

**Text Clue**
Latrice knew where the sun sets and rises. She used the information to find west.

**Text Clue**
Raul knew that butterflies taste with their feet. He used the information to escape from the giant butterfly

**Text Clue**
Juanita knew that crows like shiny things. She used the information to make the crow go away.

**Opinion**
Jackson learned that it is useful to know about nature.

**Write About the Text** I used notes from my chart to write an opinion about the most important thing Jackson learned.

## Student Model: *Opinion*

In my opinion, the most important thing Jackson learned is that it is useful to know about nature. He learned this from his friends.

First, Latrice found west because she knew where the sun sets and rises. Next, Raul knew that butterflies taste with their feet. He made the butterfly taste onion and it flew away. Finally, Juanita knew that crows like shiny things. She threw jewelry to make it go away.

The friends taught Jackson an important lesson. He learned the importance of nature.

## TALK ABOUT IT

COLLABORATE

### Text Evidence

**Underline** a text clue that comes from the notes. Does the clue support Miguel's opinion?

### Grammar

**Draw a box** around a pronoun. What does the pronoun refer to?

### Connect Ideas

**Circle** the two sentences in the last paragraph. Then combine them using *because*.

### Your Turn

COLLABORATE

In your opinion, which of Jackson's friends was the smartest? Why do you think that?

**>> *Go Digital!***
Write your response online. Use your editing checklist.

**?** **Essential Question**

Where can you find patterns in nature?

>> *Go Digital*

What patterns of colors and shapes do you see in the photograph? Where can you see patterns in nature? Write the information in the chart.

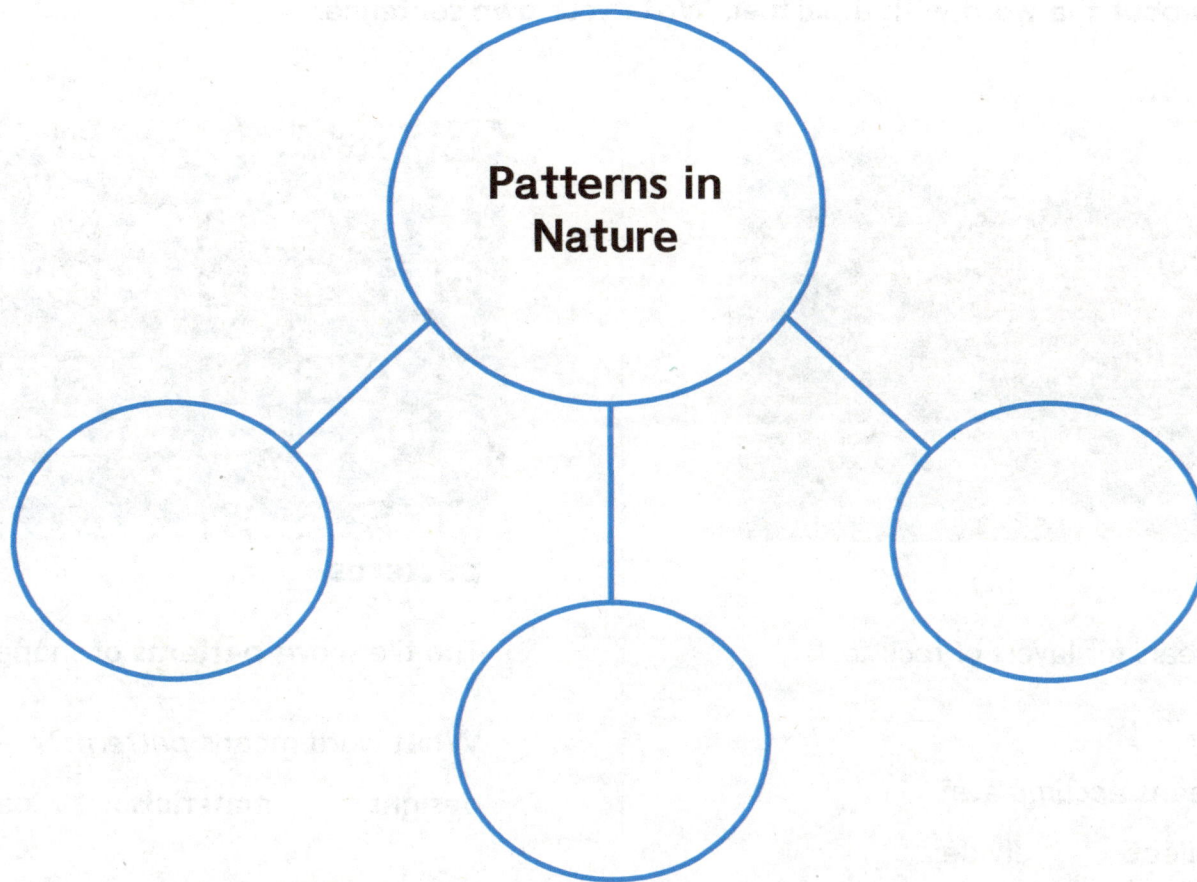

**Patterns in Nature**

Discuss the patterns you see in the salt marsh. Use words from the chart. Complete the sentences.

In the salt marsh, I see patterns of _____.

They are patterns because _____

_____.

**COLLABORATE**

**Look at the picture. Read the word. Then read the sentence. Talk about the word with a partner. Write your own sentence.**

**accumulate**

It takes many years for layers of rock to **accumulate**.

What word means *accumulate*?

**break        collect        divide**

**When does** snow **accumulate**?

Snow accumulates when _____

_____.

**patterns**

The tile shows **patterns** of shapes.

What word means *patterns*?

**designs        materials        parts**

What **pattern** does a zebra have?

A zebra has a *pattern* of _____

_____.

USGS; Westend61/SuperStock

# Words and Phrases: *in fact* and *such as*

The phrase *in fact* means "in truth" or "actually."

What is the weather like outside?

It is sunny today. But, **in fact,** it is very cold outside.

The phrase *such as* means "for example."

What does the store sell?

The store sells vegebables, **such as** tomatoes and green beans.

**Talk with a partner. Look at the picture. Read the sentence. Write the word that completes each sentence.**

It looks easy to spin the hoop, but

_____ it is hard to do.

**in fact        such as**

The aquarium has many sea animals,

_____ sharks.

**in fact        such as**

COLLABORATE

## ① Talk About It

Look at the photograph. Read the title. Talk about what you see. Use these words.

**change   rock   hill   layer**

Write about what you see.

The text is about _____

_____.

What does the photograph show?

The photograph shows _____

_____

_____.

What does the rock look like?

The rock has _____

_____

_____.

Take notes as you read the text.

# Patterns of Change

### Essential Question

**?**

**Where can you find patterns in nature?**

Read about patterns you can find in rocks and rock formations.

## Rock Solid

Rocks change. In fact, water, wind, and temperature slowly change one type of rock into another type of rock. These forces also shape the rocks that make up land.

The photograph across these pages shows an example. This rock structure is the Wave formation. It is made of sand that turned to rock over a long time.

## Igneous Rocks

Igneous rocks are one type of rock. They are formed from hot, liquid rock called magma. Magma flows far below Earth's surface, but sometimes it moves to Earth's surface through volcanoes. When this happens, magma becomes lava. Lava, or melted rock, slowly cools. Eventually, it hardens into solid rock.

There are many kinds of igneous rock. Two kinds are granite and obsidian. Granite feels rough and comes in many colors. Obsidian is smooth and often black.

Granite

Obsidian

(bkgd) Stockbyte/Getty Images; (t)sciencephoto/Alamy Stock Photo; (b)The Natural History Museum, London/Alamy Stock Photo

# Text Evidence

**1 Specific Vocabulary** 🅐🅒🆃

Reread the second sentence in the third paragraph. What is magma? Circle the words that tell you.

Magma is _____

_____.

**2 Comprehension**
**Main Idea and Key Details**

Reread the last paragraph. Underline the details that tell about igneous rock.

Granite and obsidian are _____

_____

**3 Sentence Structure** 🅐🅒🆃

Read the third sentence in the third paragraph. Underline the text that tells what magma does sometimes.

Sometimes magma _____

_____

_____

## 1 Sentence Structure **A C T**

Reread the third sentence. What do water and wind do with particles? Circle the two verbs. Write about it.

Water and wind _____

_____.

## 2 Specific Vocabulary **A C T**

The word *deposit* means "to leave something at a place." What things do water and wind deposit? Put a box around the text. Where do they get deposited? Circle the text.

**COLLABORATE**

## 3 Talk About It

Reread the fourth paragraph. Discuss what makes a stratum. Then write about it.

_____

_____

## Sedimentary Rocks

Water and wind transform igneous rock. Slowly, water and wind erode, or break apart, igneous rock. Then water and wind carry away the particles of broken rock and deposit them at places, such as a beach or a desert.

Gradually, the particles collect in layers. The layers get pressed together until they form a new material, called sedimentary rock. The materials that form sedimentary rock include rocks and sand. It can also include matter from living things, such as plants, bones, and shells.

There are different kinds of sedimentary rock. Sandstone is formed from sand. Limestone is made of bones and shells.

Limestone

## Rock Formations

Over time, a layer of one kind of sedimentary rock forms, called *stratum*. Geologists who study rocks call a layer made of the same materials at about the same time a stratum. Another stratum forms on top of the first stratum. The plural for stratum is strata.

Marble

Many strata can accumulate. The oldest layer is at the bottom. The youngest layer is at the top. Geologists learn a lot by studying the chronology of layers. The layers create patterns.

Sandstone

## The Rock Cycle

You can find a third type of rock, called metamorphic rock, below Earth's surface. Layers of rock above the metamorphic rocks press down on them. At the same time, magma heats the metamorphic rocks from below. The heat causes some metamorphic rocks to melt and become magma.

As the magma slowly cools, it turns back into igneous rock. This process is called the rock cycle. The rock cycle is a pattern that repeats and continues. It turns liquid rock into a solid. It builds cliffs from sand and bones. And it returns rock to liquid form.

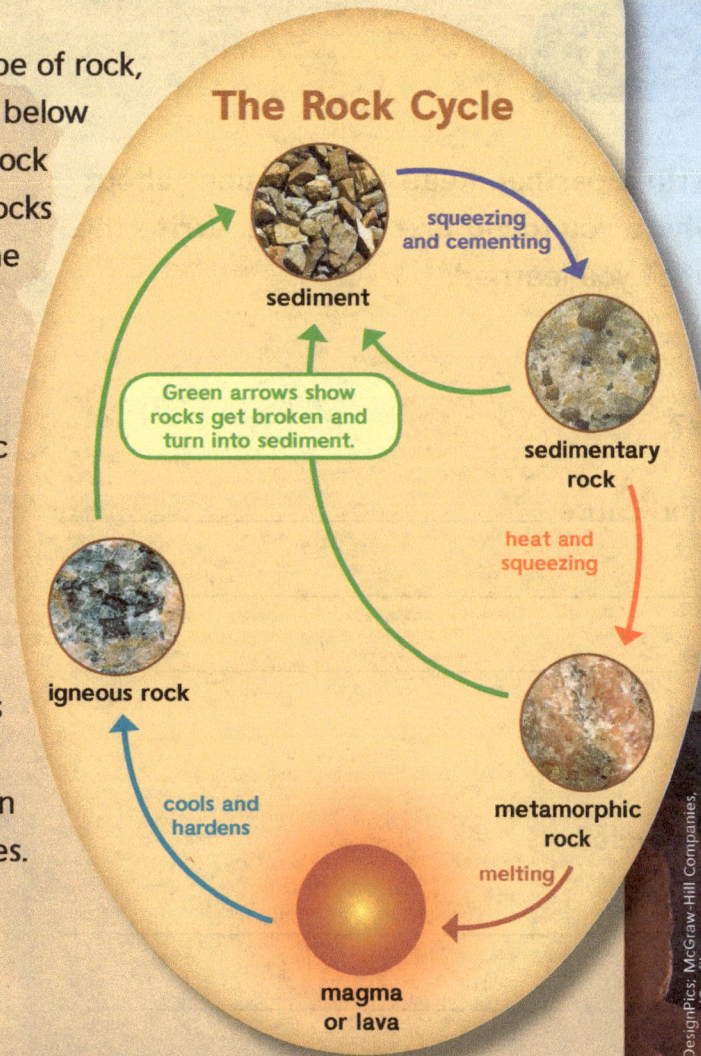

### The Rock Cycle

sediment

squeezing and cementing

Green arrows show rocks get broken and turn into sediment.

sedimentary rock

heat and squeezing

igneous rock

metamorphic rock

cools and hardens

melting

magma or lava

(bkgd) ericfoltz/iStock/360/Getty Images; (t to b) Steve Nagy/DesignPics; McGraw-Hill Companies, Inc./Bob Coyle, photographer; Doug Sherman/Geofile; Doug Sherman/Geofile

### Make Connections

**?** Talk about the patterns you can find in sedimentary rocks. Where do you see these patterns? ESSENTIAL QUESTION

Compare the patterns in rocks with other patterns you have seen. TEXT TO SELF

## Text Evidence 🔍

**1 Sentence Structure** Ⓐ Ⓒ Ⓣ

Reread the second sentence. Circle the phrase that tells about location. Where are the metamorphic rocks?

Metamorphic rocks are _____

_____.

**2 Comprehension**
### Main Idea and Key Details

Reread the second paragraph. What is the rock cycle? Put a box around three details that tell what happens in the rock cycle. Write the details.

_____

_____

_____

COLLABORATE

**3 Talk About It**

Talk about the diagram of the rock cycle. Discuss how rocks change to liquid then back to solid.

35

# Respond to the Text

**Partner Discussion** Work with a partner. Read the questions about "Patterns of Change." Show where you found text evidence. Write the page numbers. Then discuss what you learned.

**What patterns are in rocks?**

I learned that water and wind cause _____.    Page(s): _____

Strata are _____.    Page(s): _____

Layers are patterns because _____.    Page(s): _____

**Text Evidence**

**What pattern is in the rock cycle?**

First, magma _____.    Page(s): _____

Then, igneous rock _____.    Page(s): _____

Finally, sedimentary and metamorphic rock _____.    Page(s): _____

The rock cycle is a pattern because _____

_____.    Page(s): _____

**Text Evidence**

**Group Discussion** Present your answers to the group. Cite text evidence for your thinking. Listen to and discuss the group's opinions.

COLLABORATE

**Write** Work with a partner. Look at your notes about "Patterns of Change." Write your answer to the Essential Question. Use text evidence to support your answer. Use vocabulary words in your writing.

COLLABORATE

What patterns can you find in rocks?

Strata are layers of _____.

Strata are one kind of pattern because _____

_____.

A rock cycle is a process of _____

_____.

A rock cycle is another kind of pattern because _____

_____.

**Share Writing** Present your writing to the class. Discuss their opinions. Talk about their ideas. Explain why you agree or disagree with their ideas.

COLLABORATE

I agree with _____.

I do not agree because _____.

# Write to Sources

**Samantha**

**Take Notes About the Text** I took notes on the idea web to answer the question: *How can the flow chart of the rock cycle help me explain the text?*

pages 32–35

**Topic**

The flow chart shows the information in the text.

**Detail**

Flow chart and text have the same topic.

**Detail**

Text explains how rock changes. Flow chart shows the changes.

**Detail**

Text explains the cycle repeats. Flow chart shows the cycle.

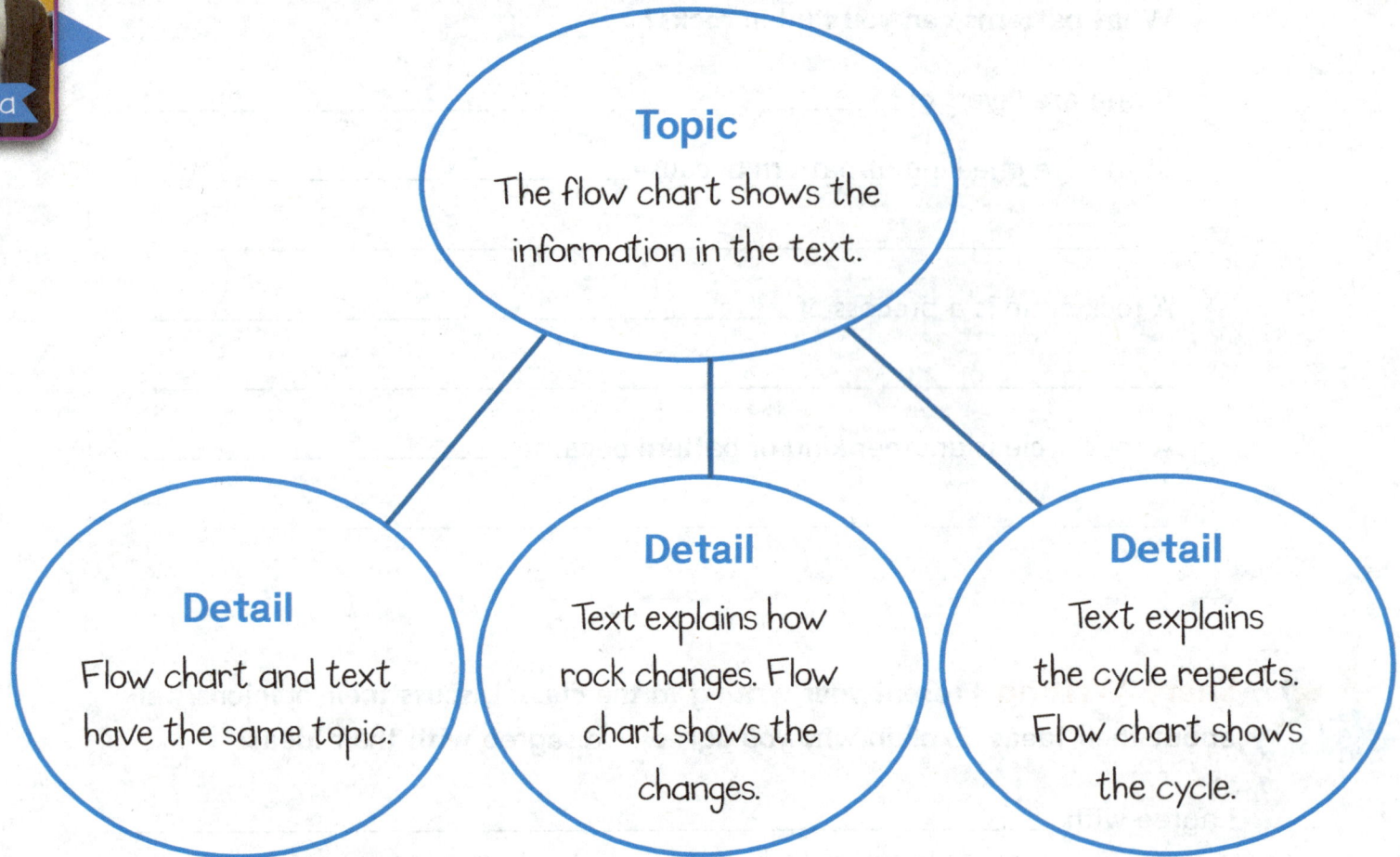

Radius Images/Getty Images

38

**Write About the Text** I used notes from my idea web to write about the flow chart.

## Student Model: *Informative Text*

The flow chart shows the information in the text. First, the topic of the flow chart and text are about the rock cycle. Then, the flow chart shows with pictures how rock changes form. For example, squeezing and cementing changes sediment into sedimentary rock. The text explains this information. Finally, the arrows in the flow chart show that a cycle repeats. The text explains that a cycle repeats.

## TALK ABOUT IT

COLLABORATE

### Text Evidence
**Draw a box** around a sentence that comes from the notes. Does the sentence provide a detail or topic?

### Grammar
**Circle** the words *flow chart*. What prepositional phrase can Samantha add to give more detail about the flow chart?

### Condense Ideas
**Underline** the two sentences about a cycle. How can you combine the sentences using *and*.

### Your Turn

COLLABORATE

What do the green arrows in the flow chart show? Use text evidence in your writing.

>> *Go Digital!*
Write your response online. Use your editing checklist.

**? Essential Question**

What benefits come from people working as a group?

>> *Go Digital*

**COLLABORATE** What are the people doing? How does working together help them? Write the ways in the chart.

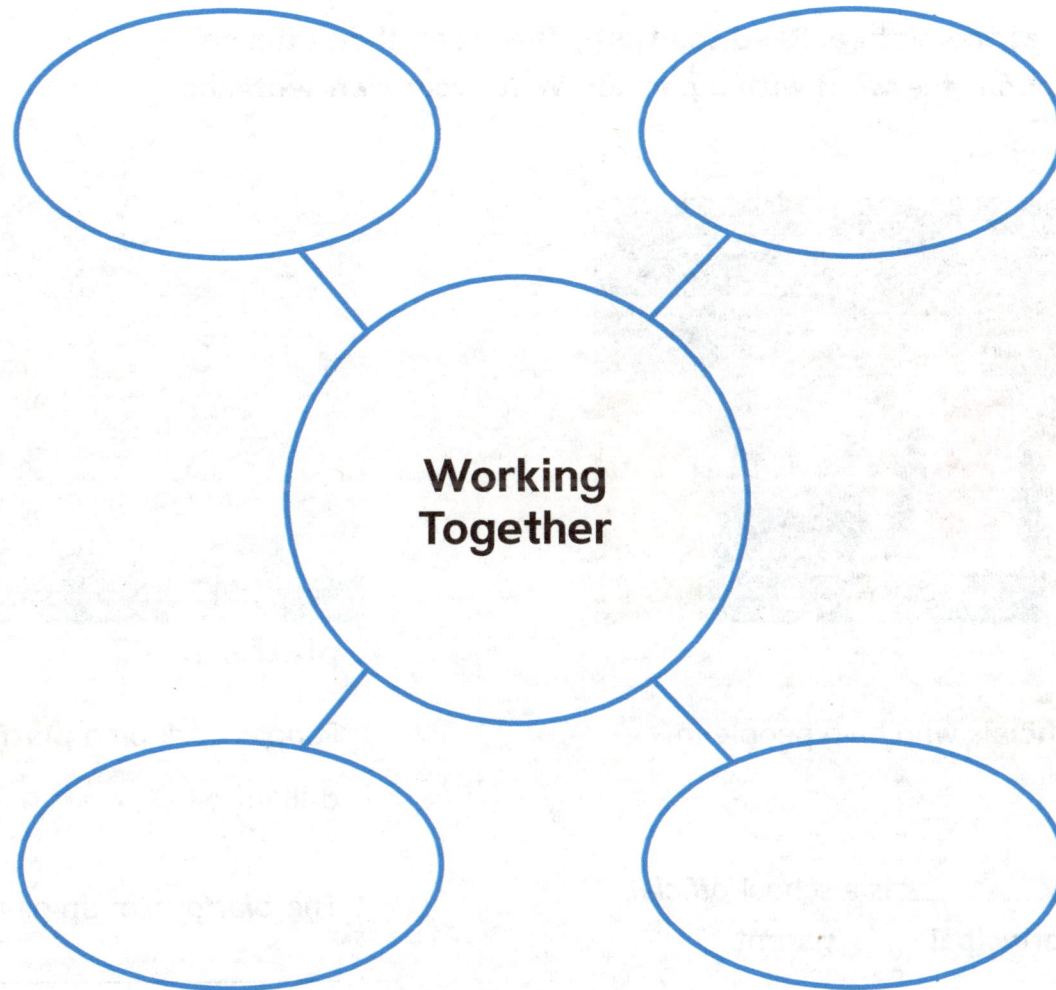

Working Together

Discuss how working together helps people. Use words from the chart. You can say:

When people work together, they can _____.

Working together helps people because _____.

# More Vocabulary

Look at the picture. Read the word. Then read the sentence. Talk about the word with a partner. Write your own sentence.

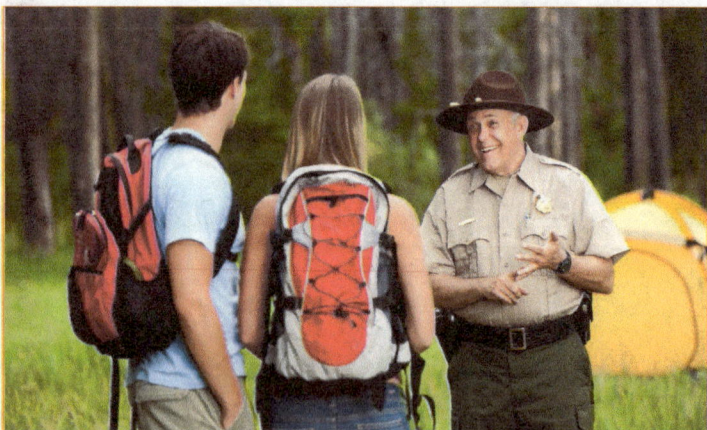

**officials**

Rangers are **officials** who help people in a park.

A _____ is a school *official*.

**student**      **principal**      **parent**

**Who are the officials at a soccer game?**

The officials at a soccer game are

_____.

**platform**

People work on a **platform** of an oil rig to drill for oil.

The *platform* of an oil rig is used by

_____.

**swimmers**      **workers**      **fish**

**What happens on a platform of an oil rig?**

Workers drill for _____ on the platform.

42

Jacom Stephens/E+/Getty Images; curraheeshutter/iStock/360/Getty Images

# Words and Phrases: Multiple-Meaning Words

One meaning of the word *well* means "successfully." The word describes a verb.

How did you do in the contest?

I did very **well**. I came in first place.

Another meaning of *well* is "a deep hole in the ground for getting oil or water."

Where do the farmers get water?

The farmers get water from the **well**.

**COLLABORATE** Talk with a partner. Look at the picture. Read the sentence. Circle the correct meaning of the word *well*.

Oil comes out of the *well*.

successfully
a deep hole in the ground

The team did *well* in the soccer game.

successfully
a deep hole in the ground

COLLABORATE

## 1 Talk About It

Look at the photograph. Read the title. Talk about what you see. Use these words.

**beach  oil  spill  together  gloves**

Write about what you see.

I see _____

_____

_____.

Where are the workers?

They are at the _____

_____.

What are the workers doing?

The workers are _____

_____

_____.

Take notes as you read the text.

# Gulf Spill Superheroes

## Essential Question

**?**  **What benefits come from people working as a group?**

Read about how groups of people worked together after the Deepwater Horizon oil spill in the Gulf of Mexico.

Often in comic books, a team of superheroes work together to solve a problem. On April 20, 2010, the Deepwater Horizon drilling **platform** exploded in the Gulf of Mexico. Fires burned above the waters. Gallons and gallons of oil spilled from a broken pipeline underwater. Teams of responders had to work together, just like superheroes in comic books.

Fire boats work to put out the fire on the Deepwater Horizon.

## Responders in the Water

Immediately after the explosion, firefighters and the U.S. Coast Guard worked to put out the fires. Boats and planes transported survivors from the platform.

Meanwhile, oceanographers mapped out the ocean floor and collected information about water currents. Biologists looked for ways to protect animals from the oil spill.

The most important part of the explosion was to fix the broken pipeline and stop the oil leak. The leak was more than a mile underwater. Engineers used robots with arms and special tools to fix the leak, but they did not stop the oil leak.

After nearly three months, workers finally stopped the leak. It took many more months to clean up the oil spill.

◀ Workers clean up some spilled crude oil at Fourchon Beach, Louisiana.

# Text Evidence

**1 Specific Vocabulary** Ⓐ Ⓒ Ⓣ

*Responders* are people who rescue others at emergencies and dangerous accidents. Circle an example of a responder in the second paragraph. What do responders do? Underline the text.

Examples of responders are _____

_____.

Firefighters _____

_____.

**2 Sentence Structure** Ⓐ Ⓒ Ⓣ

Reread the last sentence in the first paragraph. What are responders compared to? Underline the text that tells you.

**3 Comprehension**
**Main Idea and Details**

Reread the fourth paragraph. What did the workers do to stop the leak? Circle the details.

45

## 1 Sentence Structure ACT

Reread the first sentence. The sentence describes a problem and a solution. Underline the problem. Circle the solution.

The problem was _____

_____.

## 2 Comprehension
## Main Idea and Details

Reread the first paragraph. How did responders figure out where oil was spreading? Put a box around two details.

COLLABORATE

## 3 Talk About It

Reread the fourth paragraph. Discuss why fishermen needed help. Then write about it.

Fishermen needed help because

_____

_____.

## Watchers from the Sky

Responders needed to figure out where the oil was spreading, so they collaborated with other agencies to get information from the sky. The NASA space program used satellites to send information to scientists. Meteorologists tracked storms that might cause problems for the workers.

Pilots flew over the Gulf of Mexico to study how the oil spill moved. They figured out locations to put floating barriers to protect sensitive areas from oil. Other pilots transferred supplies from land to sea.

## Heroes on Land

More workers helped when the oil spill reached land. Veterinarians helped marine animals, such as pelicans and turtles. Naturalists and ecologists cleaned up the animals' habitats. Often, they helped one another.

Local fishermen also needed help. They made money selling seafood, but some seafood was not safe to eat because of the oil spill. Government officials monitored fishing areas to decide which areas were safe. Bankers and insurance companies helped the fishermen find ways to make up for the lost income.

Biologists catch a brown pelican. It is covered in oil. The biologists clean the pelican and return it back to nature.

(bkgd) Photodisc/Getty Images; (inset) Saul Loeb/AFP/Getty Images

In Florida, experts worked together to trap floating globs of oil before they reached the beaches. They created the SWORD, or Shallow-water Weathered Oil Recovery Device. The small boat had mesh bags hung between two pontoons. It worked like a pool skimmer and scooped oil as it moved.

The Deepwater Horizon accident required heroic efforts of all kinds. Each hero had his or her own job. But to solve the problem, everyone had to work well together, too.

Workers place materials to catch oil in Orange Beach, Alabama.

## Make Connections

**?** How did people work together with the responders at the site of the oil spill?
**ESSENTIAL QUESTION**

How have others helped you achieve a goal? Explain how you worked together to meet the challenge. **TEXT TO SELF**

## Text Evidence

### ❶ Specific Vocabulary Ⓐ Ⓒ Ⓣ

The word *experts* means "people who have special skills or know a lot about a subject." What is the goal of the experts? Underline the text that tells you.

### ❷ Comprehension
### Main Idea and Details

Reread the first paragraph. How did the experts work together? Circle two details. What do the details have in common?

The details describe how _____

_____

_____.

**COLLABORATE**

### ❸ Talk About It

Discuss how everyone worked together to solve the problems of the oil spill. Support your answer with text evidence.

# Respond to the Text

**Partner Discussion** Work with a partner. Read the questions about "Gulf Spill Superheroes." Show where you found text evidence. Write the page numbers. Then discuss what you learned.

COLLABORATE

---

**What did you learn about the Deepwater Horizon oil spill?**

**Text Evidence** 🔍

I read that a drilling platform _____.

Page(s): _____

Above the water, the explosion caused _____.

Page(s): _____

Below the water, oil _____.

Page(s): _____

---

**How did people work together to find solutions for the oil spill?**

**Text Evidence** 🔍

Responders needed to _____.

Page(s): _____

Responders worked with _____.

Page(s): _____

Experts made a craft that _____

Page(s): _____

_____.

---

**Group Discussion** Present your answers to the group. Cite text evidence for your ideas. Listen to and discuss the group's opinions.

COLLABORATE

**Write** Work with a partner. Look at your notes about "Gulf Spill Superheroes." Write your answer to the Essential Question. Use text evidence to support your answer. Use vocabulary words in your writing.

COLLABORATE

What benefits came from groups working together after the spill?

People needed to work together because _____

_____.

Some workers stopped the oil leak by _____.

Other workers cleaned up the oil by _____.

One benefit from the groups working together is _____

_____.

**Share Writing** Present your writing to the class. Discuss their opinions. Talk about their ideas. Explain why you agree or disagree with their ideas.

COLLABORATE

I agree with _____.

I do not agree because _____.

# Write to Sources

Yolanda

**Take Notes About the Text** I took notes about the text on the chart to answer the question: *What do you think was the biggest problem of the oil spill? Explain your response.*

pages 44–47

| Opinion | Text Evidence |
|---|---|
| I think the biggest problem was cleaning up the spill. | It was difficult to figure out where oil was spreading. |
| | Veterinarians and ecologists cleaned the animals and the habitats. |
| | Local fishermen could not catch and sell fish. |

**Write About the Text** I used notes from any chart to write an opinion about the biggest problem of the spill.

## Student Model: *Opinion*

I think the biggest problem was cleaning up the oil spill. The responders had a lot to solve. One problem was that it was difficult to see where oil was spreading. Another problem was that veterinarians, naturalists, and ecologists had to catch and clean pelicans and turtles and other animals. They needed to clean up the habitats. Finally, local fisherman could not catch and sell fish because they were not safe.

## TALK ABOUT IT

COLLABORATE

### Text Evidence
**Underline** a sentence that comes from the notes. How does this support Yolanda's opinion?

### Grammar
**Draw a box** around the phrase *had to*. What other verbs did Yolanda use to tell that an action was necessary?

### Connect Ideas
**Circle** the first two sentences of the paragraph. How can you combine the sentences using *because*?

### Your Turn

COLLABORATE

Who do you think were the biggest heroes of the Gulf oil leak? Use text evidence to support your opinion.

>> *Go Digital!*
Write your response online. Use your editing checklist.

**? Essential Question**

How do we explain what happened in the past?

>> *Go Digital*

What is the woman doing? How can the woman learn about the past by examining things from the past? Write ways you can learn about the past in the chart.

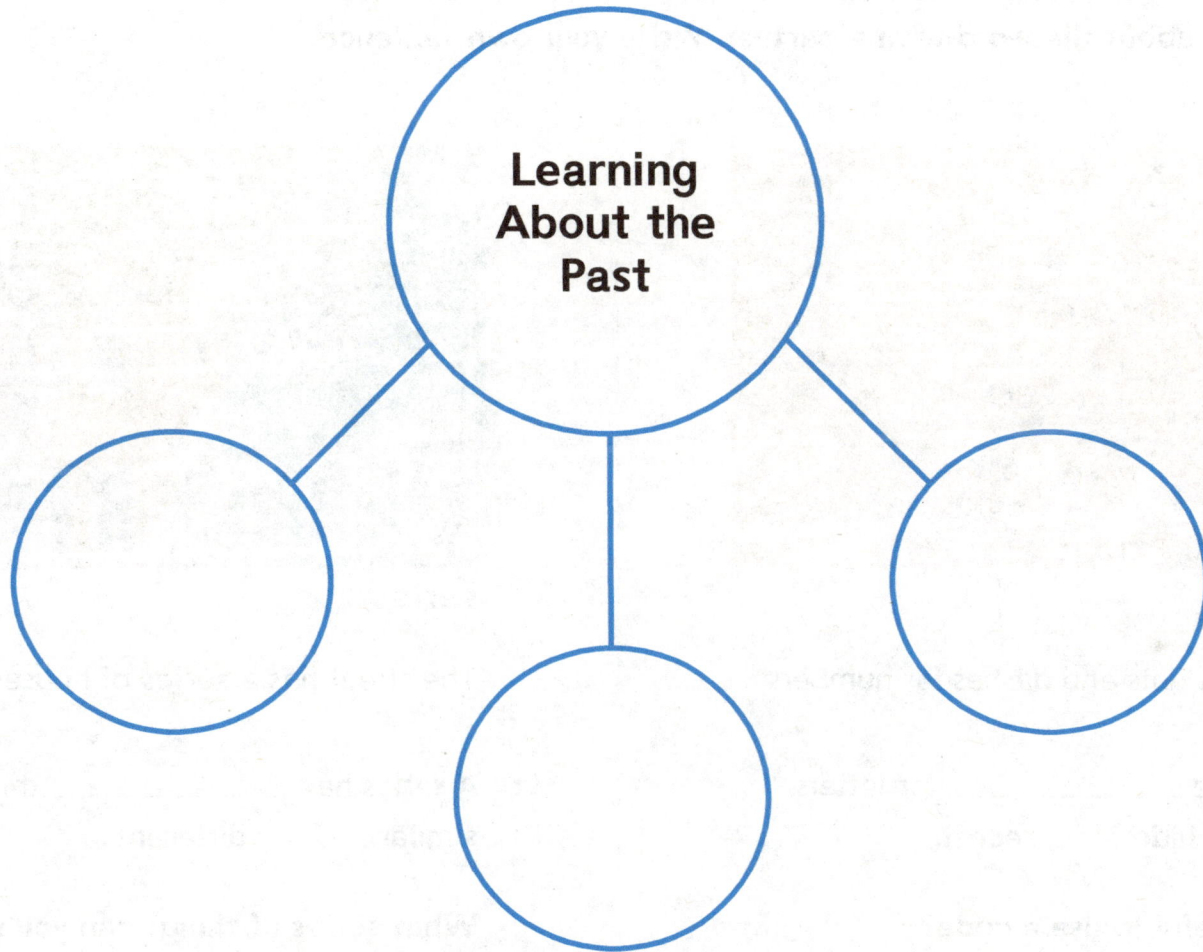

Learning About the Past

Discuss how people learn about the past. Use words from the chart. You can say:

People learn about the past by _____

_____ .

# More Vocabulary

Look at the picture. Read the word. Then read the sentence. Talk about the word with a partner. Write your own sentence.

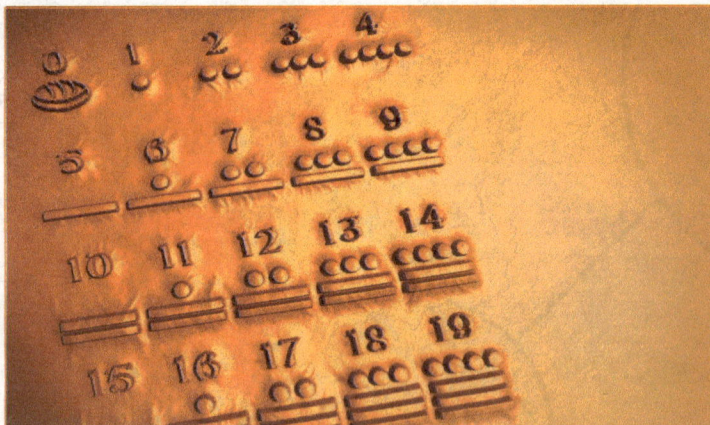

**code**

This **code** uses dots and dashes for numbers.

A code can use _____ for letters.

**symbols**        **hide**        **secret**

**When is it useful to use a code?**

It is useful to use a code when _____

_____.

**series**

The street has a **series** of houses.

A series has _____ things.

**similar**            **different**

**What series of things can you see at a garden?**

At a garden, I can see a series of _____

_____.

# Words and Phrases: *figure out* and *perhaps*

*figure out* means "to solve a problem"

What are the children trying to figure out?

The children are trying to **figure out** the puzzle.

*perhaps* means "maybe" or "possibly"

What will the family do if the trunk is full?

**Perhaps** they can put some things in an empty seat.

**COLLABORATE** Talk with a partner. Look at the picture. Read the sentence. Write the word that completes each sentence.

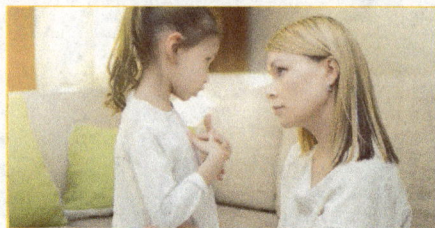

The little girl is upset. _____

she wants to play outside.

**Figure out        Perhaps**

The kids are trying to _____

how to put together the model.

**figure out        perhaps**

**COLLABORATE**

## 1 Talk About It

Look at the photograph. Read the title. Talk about what you see. Use these words.

**Inca    mountain    buildings    stone**

Write about what you see.

The text is about _____

_____.

What kind of buildings do you see?

I see _____

_____

_____.

Who lived in these buildings?

_____

_____

Take notes as you read the text.

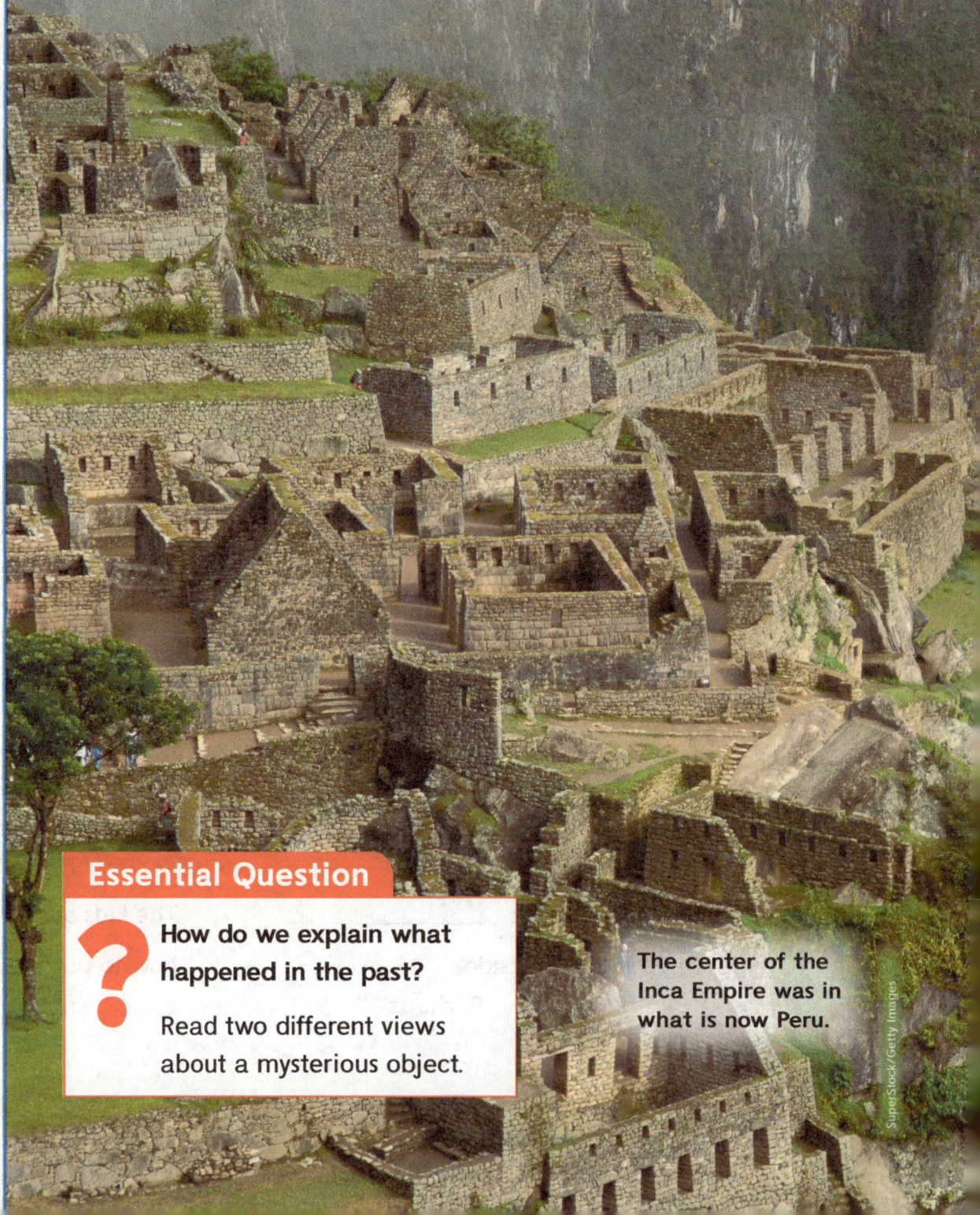

### Essential Question

**?** **How do we explain what happened in the past?**

Read two different views about a mysterious object.

The center of the Inca Empire was in what is now Peru.

SuperStock/Getty Images

# What Was the Purpose of the Inca's STRANGE STRINGS?

**POINT COUNTERPOINT**

## String Theory

### Was the quipu an ancient mathematical calculator?

Think about how difficult it is to do math problems without a calculator, paper, or pencil. The Incas were an ancient civilization in South America. They invented the quipu. It looks like a mop, but the Incas may have used it to do calculations. There are about 600 quipu that remain today.

The Incas made the quipu with wool strings attached to a horizontal cord. Both the archaeologist and the historian have tried to figure out how the quipu works. They think knots on the strings represent numbers.

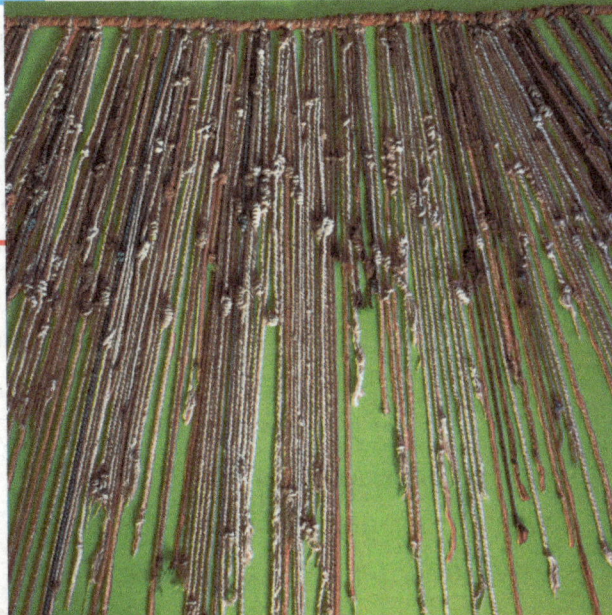

**Archaeologists are trying to figure out how the Incas used the quipu.**

It is likely that Inca officials used the quipu to record and keep data. Examples of data include the amount of crops a village produced or the number of people who lived in a house.

Stuart Franklin/Magnum Photos

**1 Specific Vocabulary** A C T

The word *ancient* means "from a very long time ago." Circle the text that gives context clues for the meaning of ancient.

**2 Comprehension**

Reread the first paragraph. What did the Incas use to do math problems? Underline the text that tells you.

The Incas may have used the quipu

to _____

_____.

**3 Sentence Structure** A C T

Reread the first sentence in the third paragraph. The sentence describes one possibility for using the quipu. Put a box around the text that describes the possibility.

One possibility is that _____

_____

_____.

57

## ① Specific Vocabulary Ⓐ Ⓒ Ⓣ

In math, *power* means "multiply a number by itself a number of times." For example, 2 to the power of 3 means 2 x 2 x 2. Circle the text that tells the power of 10.

## ② Sentence Structure Ⓐ Ⓒ Ⓣ

Reread the third sentence in the first paragraph. The sentence compares two things. Underline the text that tells you.

The sentence compares _____

_____

_____ .

## ③ Comprehension
## Author's Point of View

Reread the second paragraph. What is the author's point of view about the quipu? Put a box around the text that tells you.

The author thinks that the quipu is

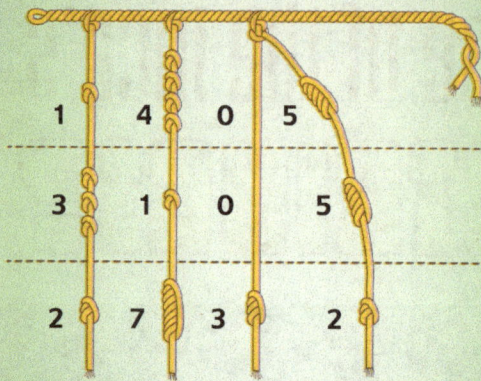

_____

_____ .

| 1 | 4 | 0 | 5 |
|---|---|---|---|
| 3 | 1 | 0 | 5 |
| 2 | 7 | 3 | 2 |

132 + 417 + 3 = 552

**Top Knots = 100s**
**Middle Knots = 10s**
**Bottom Knots = 1s**

**The illustration shows how to count with a quipu.**

This is how a quipu likely worked: Each group of knots on a string represented a power of 10, such as one, ten, and a hundred. Depending on the position of the knots, one knot could represent one, ten, a hundred, or a thousand. Clusters of knots high on a string were worth more than clusters low on a string. The Incas added the knots on a string to get a sum. They even added many quipus together.

The patterns of the knots show repeating numbers. It seems clear that the quipu was an amazing low-tech calculator.

### Counterpoint
# Spinning a Yarn

***The Incas had a language written in thread!***

Much of the Inca civilization is still a mystery. In the 1400s, the Incas built roads over the mountains, but they never used wheels. They made houses made of stone blocks that fit together perfectly. The biggest mystery may be that the Incas kept their empire together without a written language.

The quipu may be the solution to the last mystery.

**Researchers discuss a quipu.**

Many researchers think the quipu was a form of language. Researchers found seven different quipus, each with the same three-knot pattern. They think the order of the knots is a **code** for the name of an Incan city.

Researchers also found an old manuscript, a **series** of handwritten pages from the 17th century. They found the manuscript in a box that had fragments of quipu. The author of the manuscript suggests that quipus were woven symbols. The author even matched up each symbol to a list of words.

The size of the Inca empire was nearly 3,000 miles. Perhaps the quipu strings helped to keep the empire together.

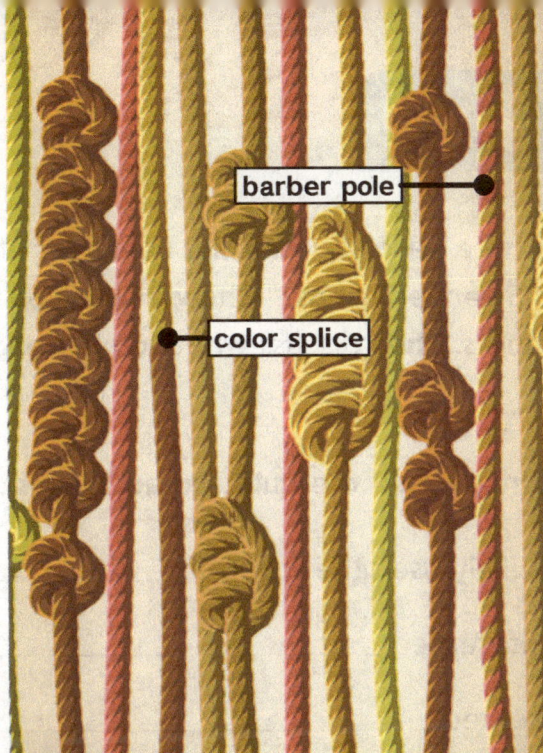

barber pole

color splice

Some experts believe that the quipu's knots were not just for counting. The quipu may reveal history.

## Make Connections

**?**

Talk about what historians found by studying the ancient quipu. **ESSENTIAL QUESTION**

Think about a time when you saw an old object for the first time. How did you find out what it was for? **TEXT TO SELF**

## Text Evidence

**1 Sentence Structure** A C T

Reread the second sentence of the first paragraph. How were the seven quipus the same? Underline the text that tells you.

COLLABORATE

**2 Talk About It**

Reread the second paragraph. Discuss why the manuscript was important. Support your answer with text evidence.

The manuscript was important

because _____

_____

_____ .

**3 Comprehension**
**Author's Point of View**

Reread the third paragraph. The author thinks the quipu was important to the Inca empire. Put a box around the text that tells you the author's point of view.

# Respond to the Text

**Partner Discussion** Work with a partner. Read the questions about "What Was the Purpose of the Inca's Strange Strings?" Show where you found text evidence. Write the page numbers. Then discuss what you learned.

COLLABORATE

**Why do people think the Incas used the quipu to add numbers?**

I read that the Incas most likely used the quipu to _____.

Each knot on the quipu represented _____.

Each group of knots represented _____.

**Text Evidence** 🔍

Page(s): _____

Page(s): _____

Page(s): _____

**Why do people think the quipu was a form of language?**

Researchers found _____.

They think the pattern of knots is _____.

An old manuscript suggests that quipus were _____.

**Text Evidence** 🔍

Page(s): _____

Page(s): _____

Page(s): _____

**Group Discussion** Present your answers to the group. Cite text evidence for your thinking. Listen to and discuss the group's opinions.

COLLABORATE

**Write** Work with a partner. Look at your notes about "What Was the Purpose of the Inca's Strange Strings?" Write your answer to the Essential Question. Use text evidence to support your answer. Use vocabulary words in your writing.

**How do we explain what happened in the past?**

Some people think the Incas used the quipus as a calculator because _____

_____

_____.

Other people believe that the Incas used the quipus as language because

_____.

We hope the quipu will tell us more about _____

_____.

**Share Writing** Present your writing to the class. Discuss their opinions. Think about their ideas. Explain why you agree or disagree with their ideas. You can say:

I agree with _____.

I do not agree because _____.

# Write to Sources

pages 56–59

**Take Notes About the Text** I took notes about the text on the chart to answer the question: *Why do some researchers think that quipus were a kind of language?*

Marta

### Text Clue
Seven quipus had the same pattern. Researchers think the pattern was a code for a city name.

### Text Clue
A manuscript from the 17th century told that quipus were symbols and matched up the symbols with words.

### Conclusion
Quipus were a kind of written language.

62

**Write About the Text** I used notes from my chart to write an informative text about the quipus.

## Student Model: *Informative Text*

Some researchers say that quipus were a written language. Two discoveries support their idea. First, researchers found the same patterns of knots on different quipus. The researchers believe the knots tell the name of an Incan city. Second, researchers found a manuscript from the 17th century. The author wrote that quipus were symbols. The author matched the symbols to a list of words. These are both strong reasons. These reasons are why some researches think quipus were a written language.

## TALK ABOUT IT

COLLABORATE

### Text Evidence

**Circle** evidence that comes from the notes. Why is this evidence important?

### Grammar

**Underline** a present-tense verb. Circle a past-tense verb. When did Marta use present-tense verbs? When did Marta use past-tense verbs?

### Connect Ideas

**Draw a box** around sentences that tell about the symbols. How can you join the sentences using the word *and*?

### Your Turn

COLLABORATE

What do other researchers believe the quipus were used for? Use text evidence to support your answer.

>> *Go Digital!*
Write your response online. Use your editing checklist.